# Breathe

Reflections & Poetry from the 2020 Lockdown

## Tumkeen

Foreword by Na'ima B. Robert

RELEASE

*Published by Release Press*

Release Press
Mirfield
WF140QZ
UK

Copyright © Release Press 2020
Cover design by Poole Publishing Services, LLC

ISBN: 978-1-913478-95-7

*Dedicated to Baba and Ami— my first fans.*
*And to my husband and children— the loudest ones.*

# Table of Contents

# *Foreword*

One of the miracles of Nature is the caterpillar that goes through a metamorphosis and emerges as a butterfly, beautiful and brilliant. This is the best way to describe the growth journey of the author of this collection, Tumkeen, as a writer and as a woman.

Word by word, paragraph by paragraph, article by article, she looks in the mirror, closely, bravely, unflinchingly, and shares the treasures she finds with us, her readers.

*And what better time to choose introspection than during a global lockdown?*

I hope that, as you read through these pages, you will discover the layers that make up Tumkeen, the woman, the mother, the writer, the seeker. And I hope that, as you read, you will discover the layers of yourself and peel them back, one by one, to get back in touch with yourself.

Na'ima B. Robert
*Award-winning author*

# Introduction

## Day Thirty

It's been a month.

It's been a month since my children have been home from school.
A little over a month since we realized how fast and how serious this virus can be.
It's been a month since I have left the house.
Since I began my self-imposed 30-day challenge to write about finding the positive, the good, and the blessings during these tough times. It's been a month of healing.

It was easy... until it wasn't.

Early days of optimism diminished fast. There were raw moments of uncontrolled anxiety that would sneak in most unexpectedly. Many times when my mind made plans to withdraw and succumb to negativity and fear. So many moments of worry and panic.

But there was only so much I could bear. How would I be able to survive? Help my family survive too?

*There's only one way out,* I thought. As I lay awake in my bed in the middle of the night, I surrendered my panic to God. And began seeking the answers from within.

I asked myself, "If you are truly at the end of your life Tumkeen, how do you want to spend it? If this virus takes you to your grave, what would you regret?" *What would I miss? What would I have wanted to do?*

And at that moment I learned that I wanted the courage to live a life rich with contentment. To be finally at peace with who I am, as I am.

I woke up every morning with the intent to let *Allah* guide my pen like a lighthouse calling all my uncertainties to shore. Riding the waves of buried emotions, through the winds of regret and guilt. I think of how the sea has been unstable and unkind, and how I am withered by it. And now, as I dock, I am finally ready to build my home.

A home that is leaving low self-esteem and depleted confidence at sea. I am releasing the ships of people-pleasing and striving for acceptance to the open waters.

I am not going back.

My final abode in this world is in the warm sands of being at peace with uncertainty. It is constructed with walls of contentment, hope, gratitude, and patience. The wall of patience is not as sturdy but it leans on others until it grows stronger with time and experience. And they all rest under the ceiling of faith. Faith gives shelter to all elements. And this is the fortress I call home now.

Each morning my pen has mapped a course that seemed as mysterious to me as others but at the end of following that trail, I have always come back to where I wanted to live... to my home on the sandy shores.

These 30 days of writing in lockdown have been an experience of a lifetime for me. It has given me perspective and clarity. And whenever I start losing my way, it takes a blaring ambulance rushing to the hospital nearby, to remind me why we are in this state. I haven't forgotten for a second the burning wildfire that still lingers around us. But while I wait for it to either catch me or extinguish, I am staying safe in my new home.

On Day One, when I began my lockdown diary, I was mobilized by a movement to find gratitude, even in the most uncertain times. But this movement became so much more. It became a journey of self-discovery and reflection to find my home. A home of peace and resolve. A home to breathe.

And I'm not going back.

# Week One

# Testimony

let closed doors
    force open the gates of your heart
let shutdown places
    broaden your mind to endless possibilities
let cancellations
    occupy you with meaningful belonging
let books of history testify
    that this was the worst of times
this was the best of times

# Day One

Yesterday was the first day.

Yesterday reality hit, "Dear God, is it ONLY day 1?!"

The kids have been home for only one day since the schools closed down.

There was arguing, there was whining, and there was fighting.

There was noise... LOUD noise, echoing throughout the house.

This was all before lunch.

But as we started settling into our day we realized we needed to set daily goals. Not an hour by hour rigorous schedule (as suggested by social media newsfeeds).

Our goals would include schoolwork, chores, and playtime. They would have screen time, meals, and snacks.

But there was also journaling.

We decided that every day we would take a break from the hustle for five minutes (setting a timer for it) and write in our journals.

Gratitude journals, to be exact.

The kids and I decided to write three things we were grateful for.

We would take pause and reflect on the things we DO have right now and the things we often overlook.

Like the love of smelling chocolate chip cookies, freshly baking on a cold winter evening.

The sound of laughter and the sight of tears when the kids gave Mom or Dad an unexpected gift on *Eid* morning.

The blessing of having each other, under this roof, safe and sound.

It took just 5 minutes of pause for all of us to feel grounded and walk away with a little smile.

I'm not going to lie, I have wanted to implement this for some time now.

It took a global pandemic for us to discover the gift of gratitude, together.

# Day Two

I am barely holding on.

Positivity wasn't as abundant today as it was yesterday.

I woke up three times last night anticipating the sound of an alert buzzing on my phone.

Something that would warn me that doom was lurching at my front door.

Of course, this led to a morning of moodiness that included snappy and grumpy.

Since then, I've been barely holding on.

Today the rope of gratitude that had previously been plenty and strong, thinned out to a weary thread.

And I'm barely able to keep it grasped.

Yet, as I vowed to myself at the start of this quarantine, I am mustering up the little positivity I do have into finding the good.

Today I am grateful for just holding on. Not letting go. Not giving up. Not hiding away from vulnerability as I desperately want to.

Sometimes just being present and showing up in whichever state I'm in is a victory for that day.

So today I am showing up; and for that I am grateful.

# Keep

Has death found you yet?

      No? Keep going

Has your breath betrayed you yet?

         No? Keep going

Have your desires melted away yet?

           No? Keep going

Has your voice lost itself to silence yet?

              No? Keep going

Has the curtain been raised to infinity yet?

                No? Keep going

Has tearful agony yearned for its love yet?

                  No? Keep going

Until the brisk breeze has chilled you,

                    keep going

While you still occupy the spaces of your limbs,

              until the sun sets in,

        keep going

      keep going

     keep going

  Until you cease,

keep on going.

# Day Three

I am now realizing that this lockdown is a marathon.
When we first heard about Michigan's COVID19 cases last week, we had a "race" mentality.
That we would all run out to the stores and buy enough toilet paper to build a fort we can hide in.
We would get food, medication, and sanitizers to take care of ourselves.
It would be over before we knew it, and we'd be okay.
But this one is different...
Beyond the snowstorms, we know how to ride out.
Beyond hurricanes that make landfall down south and reach us as thunderstorms.
Beyond blackouts and flu seasons and tornado sirens.

This one is different.

This one requires us to let go of all norms and embrace uncertainty; to become comfortable with patience; to let both fear and hope reside in vacant spaces of our home, and be okay with it all.
Because we are jogging a marathon that has only begun.
There is nowhere to take shelter or shade. Even the sanctuaries have locked their doors.
No technology or advances in science are going to help us in our course. The planes have grounded. The borders are closing. And the roads are deserted.

Nothing can make us go faster or slower than the speed we are meant to travel in this marathon.

Alienated from everyone, we are left with ourselves. Left with our patience, faith, hope, and the stamina to get us through.

Blaming no one and relying on nothing.

Just us and the path we must travel until the end appears, whichever way that may be.

Just us and the marathon.

# Day Four

I woke up to a sky that could not decide which weather it would host.
From the kitchen windows, thick gray clouds consumed the early morning atmosphere.
But at the front of my house, the sun beamed over the front lawns of homebound neighbors.
And there stood the metaphor of life that unifies each living person who is alive today.
The battle of happiness of the everyday moments versus fear of uncertainty that draws nearer and nearer.
Hope that lifts with the morning sunrise, and worry that overcasts like the dark clouds of rain.
Both sides exist, but which window will be the one that you sit by?
The one that makes living easier and bearable?
Or the one behind which heaviness looms and suffocates?

I choose to remain by the windows that filter light.

Light that spreads far and vast on this sunny spring morning.
Light that warms my home with life and newness.
Light that inspires bright red birds to perch upon the budding tree outside my door and chirp harmoniously.
I choose to see the brightness. I choose to see the light.

The dense clouds still remain on the other side of my home. And they may possibly pour loud and heavy rains against my back windows. I have no control over it.

Nor can I control the sun.

I can only control which window I choose to sit by.

I choose the light.

# A Gift

Time.
to love and be loved,
to smile,
share laughter,
to sit awhile and
stare.

Time.
to play games,
and break into giggles,
to look longer,
to drink in,
moments passed too soon.

Time.
to remain my babies,
for a second longer,
before life's fell swoop,
chases them far,
from the home of their innocence.

Time.
like a gift,
wrapped in worry,
bowed with illness,
a present,
to cherish a moment long awaited for.

Time
to live and be alive,
amid defining moments,
a space between words,
pause to breathe,
and relish,
that fleeting gift of
Time.

# Day Five

No matter where I look, the news is all about numbers.
How many days or weeks are we ahead of a country?
How many infected? How many serious cases?
The death toll.
The number of hospital beds and the number of ventilators.
Ages. Percentages. Weeks. And days.
It's all numbers, all the time.
It's just too much.
So I decided to focus away from counting numbers, to moments that count.
With that idea in mind, I have been asking myself, "If I were given a prognosis of two weeks to live, what would matter most to me... what would count the most?"
Thinking this way allows my mind to filter the numbers I have no control over.
The ones that will likely rise to uncomfortable highs... they already have.
It lets me keep the math simple.
If my days were numbered, what would I do in my day? Which actions would give me infinite contentment? How could I multiply the finite moments to last an eternity?

What would count the most?

As the days in lockdown begin to mount, this is where my focus will be.

Away from the news that will surely be counting the falling leaves, and towards the moments that count. Towards counting my blessings. Treasuring my family. Holding fast to my precious faith and not letting go.

To strive towards my many ambitions at a hurried pace.

Because in these moments of tallying the dead and dying, I choose to be at peace knowing that my days always have been and always will be finite.
It is in these finite hours I choose to multiply my time by shifting my focus towards what I value.
And to remind myself, that the numbered days I live fully are more worthy than a lifetime of fear and regret.

In the end, that is what will count the most.

# Day Six

Spring has always been my favorite time of year.

After the long cold slumber of winter, its brush of life brings color and birth to all of nature.

Trees no longer look like dry thorny branches, gray and lifeless.

They begin to show signs of life.

Little buds promise the birth of new leaves and fruit begins to emerge from them.

The faint shade of red whispers from the tall shrubs.

There is a hint of green shading the ground that was once cold, hard, and frozen.

There are signs of the changing season everywhere that I look.

A season that waits for no pandemic.

Waits for no quarantine nor lockdown.

Spring waits for no one.

It will not stop its course because the forecast calls for an abrupt cold front tonight.

If it snows, as predicted, the dogwood trees will let the snow rest awhile on top of their budding leaves that will glisten green silently from underneath.

The growth will continue even among cold fronts and wintry precipitation.

The plan of life and the season of spring will run on course as planned, as willed.

It knows that warm days will be ahead soon.

That those tiny buds will bloom with beauty in full.
It knows that the air will soon carry the quiet buzz of bees and the murmuring of flies.
That the freeze is not permanent. Not forever.
That there will be a day after.
It knows that warmth is beyond the horizon where the abundant sunshine waits to debut.
It has placed full faith in the great plan that brings it into being every year.

And like spring, I place my trust in the plan.

# Weary Eyes

sparkling stars shine light
on the weary eyes
let radiance permeate
slumbering dreams
twinkling that pours awe
into thirsty eyes
guiding from the darkness
all the lost sights
sprinkling glimmers of hope
upon the weary eyes

# Day Seven

I woke up today with fear and anxiety weaved over my head like a
cap too tight.
It was snug and uncomfortable.
Pressed on my mind with subtle force.
I could've gone on with my morning routine, but the discomfort
lingered.
So I sat down.
And held space for my fears.
I let them have a voice... have a say.
We conversed.
An intimate exchange to get to the root of my fears.

*What am I afraid of?*

Getting sick? My loved ones getting sick? Fear of dying? Fear of the
afterlife?
Yes, yes, yes, and yes.
These fears are as true as my other emotions.
Pushing them aside only gives temporary relief. It doesn't decrease
them. They still cook to thickness deep inside.
So I let them climb out of the shadows they lurk in and gave them a
seat at the table.
As we talked back and forth with each other I realized that fear will
always exist.
I cannot wish it away.

But how much space I let it hold will define if it will dominate or coexist with my other emotions.
While I let it have its say today, and acknowledged its concerns, I also let it know that it cannot be the only one I give my attention to. Like an unruly child who needs discipline and boundaries, I let fear know that it can stay as long as it remains within its boundaries.

Fear can have a room, but not the house.

# Narrow Streets

upon these narrow streets,
empty cars sit in quiet,
hibernating in solitude,
lives that have nowhere to be,

needed places sit patiently,
for weathers to calm and pass,
anxiously awaiting the morning,
an aftermath of uncertainty.

deserted cars, fancy and new,
lined into obedient columns,
hoping for their master's command,
prized useless chariots.

without pomp or purpose,
row, upon row, upon row,
irony stares so blatantly,
upon these narrow streets.

# Week Two

# Mothers

We are mothers.
Lighthouses that guide stray hearts back home,
Anchors that keep wandering minds grounded,
We are ships that flow into new waters smoothly,
Tepid currents that glisten under the blazing sun,
We ride where the wind takes us,
Cling tightly in turbulent times not letting the storm win,
We are the open arms of a vast shore ready to embrace,
We are docks that fasten our rope and never let boats go astray,
Give refuge when shelter is sought under the blanket of our waves,
Nurture existence in the deep womb of our sea,
Let little toes dip in our pool for cautious curiosity,
We are what we need to be in whichever form that it takes,
In guidance and guardianship,
We are the ocean and all its elements.
We are mothers.

# Day Eight

As a mom, my planner and phone calendar used to be filled with doctor's appointments, reminders, alerts for early dismissals, and late pickups.
It would tell me that my high schoolers had after school clubs.
Colored blocks indicating weekend events. Dinners. Plans.

But all that changed last week.

The notification alerts on my phone no longer prompt me to grab my keys to head out the door.
They are just nuisances that are quickly swiped out.
They don't ring a mental bell. They don't jolt me to get going.
In a moment, in the new reality we are all living in, none of those things matter. Not right now, at least.

All those blocked out times are free spaces.
Free to forget the world we belong to outside these walls.
Free from commitments and obligations.

Free from urgency.

Now here we are, with only each other and the time that would be loaned out to the outside, reserved only for ourselves.
We are suspended into a pause.
Like a movie where everything in the background freezes and only the actors keep moving forward.

Paused are the nuisances that take away from our lives, our time. The obligations we commit to because so are the needs of life. But we still move forward. Forward with who we are as human beings. Forward with peace and contentment. Forward with joy and love. Forward with faith.

Eventually, schools will open again. Offices and shops will be back in service. Calendars will fill in quickly with overdue check-ups and visits. And this pause will be set back to play.

Who we are when we emerge from the pause, will compose how our story plays out.

Will we return to who we were before all of this, unchanged? Will this lull cause us to remain still, fearing growth and change? Or will we move forward with better versions of ourselves? Full of resilience, hope, and second chances. Full of gratitude.

Dear lockdown, thanks for the pause.

# Day Nine

Historically, our world has been very selective in who we pray for, who we mourn.

We've prayed for certain countries and turned a blind eye to the others burning down.

We've cried over the death of some people, and forgotten about the rest.

There has been trauma and turmoil afflicting all regions, all religions, and all races.

But we cherry-picked who we wished to see ourselves in; which world resembled ours; what we allowed to "hit home."

Home is where the heart is, right?

Even when the coronavirus began making the news, it wasn't "our" problem. It affected "them."

Then when it started rippling from one continent to another, it was tragic but (phew) it wasn't happening here.

And then it landed.

Right on our rooftops.

Making our country just another one on a world map of red.

Seems like it took only a minute, then they became us, we became them.

This virus has united humanity like no catastrophe or tragedy has united us before.

It is us—all of us—against an invisible agent.

It has silently trespassed borders and boundaries like they do not exist.

If a virus can treat all of humanity as equals, then why can't we?

Why have we pushed our humanity to the side?
Our empathy out the door?
When did we get selective about whose life to mourn and whose to forget?
We are still doing it, aren't we?
Comparing if we have it as bad as other countries "out there"?
Comparing states? Comparing counties?
"What was her age?" when someone notifies us of a death.
"Any pre-existing conditions?" like that gives someone's death merit.
Anything to divide "us" from "them."
Now here we are, different to each other but the same bait to this virus.
To the virus, we are all the same in our humanity—if only we saw it that way as well.

# The Lucky Few

We'd always be the lucky few,
The ones who happened to make it through,
We fought battles like a courageous crew,
Somehow knowing what we had to do,
Patted ourselves for making it through,
Though reasons changed, reasons renewed,
Our beliefs would forever come true,
We'd always be the lucky few.

Wild ones never to be entrapped in zoos,
Able to roam the jungles as the free do,
Sidestepped the traps like we just knew,
Survivors, like the tried and true,
Risen to ranks like a valiant crew,
Smell of victory always seemed new,
Brave lions who would endlessly pursue,
We'd always be the lucky few.

The class of the few, one day saw truth,
That no one remains, we all fall through,
Time had run out so we bade adieu,
Gave space to the new ones to make debut,
Fresh faces that smell of something new,
Arrogant strides as their ignorance grew,
If only they saw, if only they knew,
We too thought we'd be the lucky few.

# Day Ten

It has been two weeks.

Two weeks since my friend texted me that "this thing" is about to get real.
That I should start stocking up with three weeks to a month's worth of non-perishables and supplies.
Two weeks since the schools sent the kids home with backpacks full of books and materials.
Two weeks since that knot of uncertainty in my stomach came into being.
Tightening with each passing day.
Two weeks since my visiting parents left to go back to their place.
Two weeks since I hugged my mom a little tighter, unsure when I would do that again...if I would do that again.
Two weeks since we realized that what "could" happen, just did.
It has been two weeks of living the (what we thought was) unimaginable.
Two weeks since I started using the word "quarantine" so often, it's the first "Q" word my phone suggests.
Two weeks since toilet paper was officially added to "America's most wanted" list.
With hand sanitizer a close second.
Two weeks since plans got canceled and appointments postponed.

Indefinitely.

Two weeks since life pressed pause.
Yet continues to play out, in a realm only sci-fi fanatics could imagine.
Two weeks.
It feels like it's been a whole other lifetime.

Yet,

I am filled with gratitude that I have spent the past two weeks with my family.
Safe and secure.
Still eating, sleeping, playing, and praying.
Living.
It's been two weeks since I learned what gratitude actually means.
And how it is the foundation that keeps me grounded.
It's been two weeks since gratitude became the home-remedy of living in quarantine.

# Day Eleven

Today is *Jummah*, and today I am mourning. Grieving.

Lost.

Yes, I know it is temporary and soon our *masjid* will be bustling once again.
But right here, right now, I am feeling an intense sense of grief.

Empty.

I am grieving the busy hustle Friday brings. I am grieving the etiquette of joining *Jummah* prayers. I am grieving the joy *Jummah* has brought me.
It's always been the culmination of a week's happiness, rejoiced on one single day.
I miss the smell of attar and crisp clothes wafting in the morning like an air of celebration.

We make our best food on *Jummah*. We laugh a little more. And smile a whole lot.
The food will still be made. But the mood will not be there.
Yes, there are live streams and speeches at my fingertips.

It's not the same.

I don't feel the same. We don't feel the same.

My kids would hear from me about *Jummah* preparations the night before, the morning of, and at school pickup.

And now they feel that same loss, the same grief.

"I keep feeling like we have somewhere to go."

We do. It's where the heart yearns to be. Where aching hearts feel contentment. Where we rejoice. Where we are reminded of our brotherhood and community. It is our home.

It is the House of Allah where we are invited for a special day of celebration.

It feels like the invite has been rescinded.

The house is closed. The lot is empty. And our hearts are mourning.

Everything that has ever meant anything is now clearly in focus.

The places we took for granted. The routine we thought was boring.

The days that we commemorated more out of habit than intention.

The very breaths we let escape as sighs of disappointment.

That breath is now more precious than ever before.

And on this Friday, as we follow the *sunnah* of the day without going to the *masjid,* my heart is left with a hunger that can only be satiated upon our return there.

I am grateful for the heart that aches for the blessed *Jummah* prayers like it never has before.

# Hold Me

Hold me tight
I am limp with fear,
Don't know if I have
The strength to bear,

Hold me tight
I tremble with worry,
I have much time
But I feel the hurry,

Hold me tight
I am too frail to see,
Beyond the smoke
Past the fury,

Hold me tighter
I surrender to truth,
Fasten me firmly
Hold me close to You.

# Day Twelve

Yesterday was tough.

There were tears. There was sadness.
It was a down day.
I didn't want to be positive or find joy in anything.
I made that decision.
And gave myself permission.
I imagine that this lockdown may make days like yesterday a regular occurrence.
Days when staying afloat is the only thing I have the energy for.

When taking a deep breath requires effort.
When tears remain at the corners of my eyes.
When the heart mourns for days past not too long ago, that wasn't as heavy as these days feel.

Because these days seem heavy and loaded.

Yesterday, I gave myself permission to sit on the sidelines to catch a breath.
I was winded from being needed. From being brave and strong. From holding up the fort for everyone.
So I took the load off, and shed some tears,
...on a prayer mat.
...in front of my Lord.
And I left it all there.

Today, I woke up grateful for another day.
And a chance to pick up the load that is meant for me to carry.
Because I know with certainty,

"*Allah* burdens no soul beyond what it can bear" (Quran 2:286).

# In the Gardens

Let us meet time and time again
In the gardens full of fruit,
I shall pluck them from where they beam
Sweetly fragrant, ripe with truth.

Let us meet where we always do
Where I arrive with empty hands,
You offer me to stroll and take
Always taking more than I planned.

Here I am, under the high sun
Parched by the scorch of the day,
Yet nothing can pull me aside
From the gardens where I came to stay.

The baskets are flowing with bright colors
Red, purple, and green,
But there's so much more I see out there
An abundance everywhere that I lean.

You come and press upon my shoulder
Reminding that the sun will set,
But my hands still reach for fruits ahead
With tears dripping down, I whisper "...not yet."

I drag my baskets from tree to tree
Frantic to take whatever I can,

Tired but driven to keep striving
You offer my weariness a hand.

A sudden rush of pursuit emerges
As I run to the trees in the back,
And I point to what I see in the distance
A yellow that glows against the black.

As my heart grows full with content
I sigh knowing I've gathered what I need,
I stand up from the plush velvet soil
From the gardens that nourish and feed.

# Day Thirteen

Positivity is a skill.
Practiced but never really perfected.
A journey of striving and perseverance.
Positivity is not a destination.

You never arrive.

You don't call it home to furnish and become comfortable in.
Because it requires a constant, deliberate effort.
It may be harder for some and easier for others.
Positivity is a skill that is sharpened each time you practice it.
Not because the situation isn't difficult. It is.
It is when, despite feelings of immense worry and fear, you choose
to turn the switch on and let the light in.
You know the negativity exists... it remains.
But you shift your focus to the positive.

Positivity is a lens you choose to stream your situation through.
Put into focus every time you choose to see the good.
Even in times of uncertainty. Even during a lockdown. Even during a
global pandemic.
Because the fragility of life is not dependent on the frail threads
that weave it. Rather, it relies on the tapestry that strengthens it.

Even in an impossible situation, there are those who fight for hope.
Just ask every healthcare worker who sees the potential of life even
in the weak.
Ask every mother who feels the warmth of an infinite love when she
embraces her unruly child tightly.
Ask every child who sees wonder in a puddle rather than mud and
rain.
Like seeing the protection of your home as a fort that withstands
the storm, and not a cage that prevents you from flying free.
Practice positivity not because you don't see the negative side.

Practice positivity in spite of it.

Because in a world that seems to be more chaotic than ever, a
positive mindset may be the only thing you can control.

# Day Fourteen

Hope.
Like holding a flickering candle against the compelling breeze.
It throws open the doors of an entrapped soul.
Allows the light to come in and feed it so that the soul may thrive.
It lets joy remain sheltered when impending clouds thunder on the horizon.
In troubled times, hope is as necessary for emotional existence as water is for the physical state.
Without hope, there is only the intensity of dark despair left.
Feelings that seem to sit heavy on the chest and tighten the throat.
A disparity that continually simmers, thickened with fear, and worry.
During a climate of uncertainty, I would rather lean into hope.
Hope to be safe. Hope to survive. Hope to find the good, no matter what.
Even though the strong winds of worry blow relentlessly at the small flickering light in my hand, I refuse to let the light die out.

I choose to lean into hope.

# Fires

The speed of winds has picked up,
Soon the blaze will run too deep,
Fires ravaging wildly,
A savage that swallows trees.

Unknowing wilderness watches,
Awaiting the blaze to pass,
Alone in the darkness, they sit,
Clinging to the blades of grass.

Floating sparks seem innocent,
As they perch upon the leaves,
Calmly they begin to kindle,
Leaving embers in place of trees.

The winds will gently persist,
To carry the blaze afar,
Flames that glow so brightly,
Their remains, like clumps of char.

Fires know only to burn,
Their essence is in the heat,
But just beneath the ashes,
Grow trees that deny defeat.

# Week Three

# Good Morning from my Quarantine

Good morning from my quarantine
I am awakened from my world of dreams,
to brilliance breaking from the darkened sky,
blushing clouds that push light up high,
rays that pierce hope beyond the glass walls,
melodious chatter hidden behind bird calls,
it's a morning much like the ones before,
but the gifts it brings mean so much more,
fleeting life is desperate to remain,
stolen moments are time that is gained,
there is revival in the bloom of trees,
chasing squirrels brings excited glee,
the warmth of the breeze is a gentle caress,
tingle of raindrops leaves skin refreshed,
existence energized beyond routine,
good morning from my quarantine

Good morning from my quarantine
ringing sirens are a daily routine,
prowling through streets like cats that prey,
we remain still but eyes do not stay,
as they pass us by, a deep exhale,
our scent of life didn't leave a trail,
"It could've been us," the neighbors we love,
hushly rushed by men masked and gloved,
too fast to say our last goodbyes,
eyes too afraid to even cry,

but not this time, not yet at least,
the wailing sirens were only a tease,
life can resume, we can return to play,
still meant to live, still meant to stay,
busying ourselves behind curtain screens,
good morning from my quarantine

Good morning from my quarantine
we must be on day eleventeen,
accustomed to the view from here,
some days of hope, some days of fear,
the house is cleaned, the books are read,
the food is cooked, the children fed,
quiet mornings lead to still nights,
solitude only bluntly bites,
we made amends with this way of life,
away from each other, away from sight,
counting the days to move forward again,
recovering past this crippling pain,
remembering the days when we were free,
only foreign news showed people's plea,
we lived advanced in our modern times,
they were paying for their own crimes,
but now here we are, all the same,
tallying numbers without a name,
from where we stand no grass looks green,
good morning from my quarantine

Good morning from my quarantine
what does all this really mean?

humanity shaken to its very core,
barricaded behind sealed up doors,
all we hold is time itself,
with our loved ones and stocked up shelves,
I have now, to pause and see,
what this world really means to me
have I relished the moments, the bad and the good?
did I give my all, do all that I could?
living in the present knowing death is near?
or was I chasing life out of death's cold fear?
I hope whether my life ends this day or next,
I honor the beats and breaths in my chest,
with grateful humility, in service to Him,
complete submission, every will and limb,
that beyond these days of trouble and worries,
I lettered a manual of triumphant stories,
my book handed back in glowing light,
that I kept my word and fought the fight,
these days of seclusion is my second try,
to make right my faults before I should die,
I thank Him for this pause to reflect,
to make amends and pay my respects,
for the journey to Heaven is long and great,
I am collecting provisions while I wait,
His mercy is infinite, He will help me forth,
I am awaiting my ride to depart this port,
ships carried by an army of white wings,
they enshroud me in robes sent by Him,
a glorious journey to serene,
good night from my quarantine.

# Day Fifteen

Today is the last day of March, and what a month it has been!
I could've never imagined this month would play out the way that it has... not even in my wildest imagination.
No one really could've.
All the smart people in suits and glasses on the news are indicating that April will be even more unimaginable.
Those who couldn't have predicted or prepared for devastation of this size, want us to believe them when they say it will get worse.
And maybe it will.
So what do I do in the meanwhile?
Loved ones have warned me to make an emergency preparedness plan, and keep a hospital bag ready (in case...).
I laughed.
Because as much as I love them, I found the idea to be pretty crazy.

Am I supposed to be preparing for my deathly hospital stay?

What would this bag contain anyway? When I made a hospital bag for my labor and delivery, I kept toiletries, swaddling blankets, baby clothing, and some gum.
Where is the checklist for hospital essentials when you get infected by a plague that makes you gasp for air? Should I pack my enshrouding garment to wrap my remains, just in case? Should I keep lip gloss so when I give my goodbyes on Facetime, I look presentable?!
To their dismay, I will not be preparing a bag.

But I AM preparing in my own way.

I am preparing to live even harder.

As bad as the news gets, that's how much deeper I am digging in to savor life, while I have it.
I find myself holding my husband's hand with more deliberation and affection.
Inhaling the sweetness of my children's heads intently as they embrace me.
Smiling as the squirrels run around my yard, lulling me into a trance of happiness.
Being present in the moments, like when the drops of water from my shower hit my head and pour down my back.
April may hit like a tsunami wave, but I will not be preparing for the devastation.
Nope, not me.
I will be grateful for all the moments in the meanwhile.
And live a life so hard, no wave can seize.

# Day Sixteen

Reality is settling in.
And it's somber.
This new way of life was digestible as a concept but is getting hard
to swallow as a reality.

I now get what all the hype to buy toilet paper was about—it was
panic.
I now get what all the wiped out sanitizer was about—it was fear.
The binge-watching of news and headlines—it was about shock.
The need to schedule every hour—it was about control.

However, after weeks of moving through a rush of every emotion
possible, it seems like we are becoming soberingly calm.
Calm because we as a country are now entering this new phase
called acceptance. Accepting the severity of the times we are living
in and that it's not going away soon.
Don't get me wrong: I still feel immense gratitude for what I have. I
still pray with conviction because I believe wholeheartedly in the
power of prayer.
I am positive and hopeful. Laughing and loving. I am all of these
things.

But I am human.

My humanness says that fear and worry were created in me
alongside love and faith. I am allowed to and supposed to feel all the
emotions I was born with.
They are all present, all valid.
Acceptance of this situation is as important as the acceptance of our
emotional spectrum.
Because acceptance means making peace.
Making peace with it all.
The emotions, the reality, the fragility, and uncertainty.
Making peace and being at peace.
Surges in emotions and mental state can only persist for so long.
There comes a time you accept the reality of knowing it's not in your
hands.
It never was.

And I am at peace with that.

# Ill City

My city has fallen ill,
God, will you help us please?
The air is getting tight up here,
We're finding it hard to breathe.

The burning keeps us restless,
We need You to cool us down,
Shaking so uncontrollably,
No escape from this ailing town.

My city's reach returns empty,
Hard to grasp what we need.
Time is ever fleeting,
Too many lungs to feed.

We're using masks as shelters,
To shield us from the pain.
Washing hands continuously,
To wash away the stains.

My city has been muted,
Please hear its silent screams.
They sound like blaring sirens,
Chasing peaceful dreams.

God, we are at Your mercy,
Fallen to our humbled knees.

Head bowed down before you,
Rescue us from this siege.

My city is awake tonight,
We've lulled the kids to sleep.
Turning to you with hopeful hearts,
Fighting for a chance to breathe.

# Day Seventeen

There seems to be a new popular destination on everyone's minds these days.

It's not an exotic seaside vacation or the exploration of a historic city.

The world now collectively dreams of a destination called Normal.

Everyone wants to know: How can we get to Normal? When will it be normal again? When will normality return?

Which makes me question... what is normal anyway?

Is it normal to be rushing out the door every morning to individual lives?

Dropping kids off and being by yourself for 8 hours until the children return?

Is it normal to be everywhere with everyone but rarely inside your own head?

Is it normal to be out there instead of in here?

Was it normal when conversations took place from the corner of your eye while your gaze rested on a screen?

Was it normal to be out working so late that you missed out on eating dinner with the rest of the family?

When did we decide (and who decided?) that what we *were* was the "normal"?

Minus the severity of the virus, things today seem to be a little more normal than they have been for ages.

Children are valuing the enrichment of outdoor play.
Families are sitting down together for meals again.
There seems to be more time to do the small things that bring joy,
like cooking, painting, listening, and praying.
Suddenly what is a luxury and what is necessary seems to be in
focus.
There is a little more clarity these days. Clarity on what is priority...
what *really* matters.
I wonder if "going back" to normal is truly what we seek? And if not,
what will the "new normal" look like?

Will there be jobs waiting for us still?
After being solely with their parents for weeks now, will children go
back to school as routinely as they used to?
Will members of families go back to eating at their own individual
times?
Will we forget about connecting with loved ones and go back to
scheduled lives?
Will we change? Have we already?
Will the destination we seek in the distant horizon be as glorious
when it arrives at our doorstep?

Because there was a time we used to say, "If only I had more time..."
and now we've been given just that.
There was a time when we'd ask, "Why can't we do this as a family?"
Well, we get to now.
We used to say, "Can't we just put the phone down and enjoy a
walk?" We are now.

Is the normal we want to have returned, a normal worth going back to?
Or is where we want to be a place more wise?
Because what we are aspiring to no longer exists. The naive yesterday is as gone as the March we planned out but never experienced.
The new normal will be birthed from the quarantine of today.

So sit back and reflect on what "normal" truly is.

Will this quarantine and days of solitude have made us better people who will have a better tomorrow?
Is it possible that we will survive this demanding better from ourselves because normal is no longer good enough?

Now *that* may actually *be* normal.

# Gone

Where have all the people gone?
The streets whisper their names,
Hushed roads echo in silence
It just doesn't feel the same

Empty swings gently glide
Beyond the line of trees,
Loud play and joyful laughter
Whisper softly in the breeze

Rows of abandoned lots
Vast but in muted despair,
Hollowed buildings cast dark shadows
Longing as they silently stare

Cities that bustled with people
Left deserted without a trace,
Traffic lights with signals still flashing
To the memory of a crowded space

The twinkling glow of a life at night
Once gave way to a coming dawn,
Now dimmed in the still of darkness...
Where have all the people gone?

# Day Eighteen

The irony of reaching into gratitude even deeper in worrisome times is not lost on me.

After all, how can we find ourselves to be more positive when there is a plague creeping up on every side of this world?

We see the news. We see the numbers. We see the faces. The suggestive language that is heavy with negativity.

How then is gratitude even more necessary?

How does gratitude help?

Let me tell you something, I have been through dark times before. No, nothing like this plague, but emotionally and mentally I have lived in a dark place before.

A dark place that was the only space for a long time. I have felt sadness so deep that all I could see was despair. Loneliness. Hopelessness.

It became so ingrained in me that I forgot who I had been before it. I lived a lifetime there.

And then I turned 40, and something stirred in me. A need for change.

Like a median in the middle of a busy street, observing cars that are driving back and those that were rushing forward.

There I was stuck in between, deciding if I wanted to go back to a familiar, dark world, or push forward to a new, uncomfortable realm.

I decided to push forward.

And since then, I have satiated my appetite to live better and bolder by weaving hope and gratitude into the fabric of me.
I will no longer let darkness scare me into a corner heavy with the shadows of despair.

No more.

As the current situation taps into those same feelings of fear, worry, and uncertainty, I will continue to prescribe for myself the opposite of that mindset: I will continue to take a heavy dose of gratitude.
Grateful for finding solace in prayer and meditation. Grateful for the heartbeats. Grateful for the breaths. Grateful for love and joy. The list really is endless.
Don't get me wrong, I am not so far ahead in my journey that fear doesn't touch me anymore. Not so forward that worries don't pull me a few steps back.
They do. They always will. When you've hit rock bottom before, there is a natural tendency to gravitate towards that out of habit.
But I refuse to be pulled back. I persist.
As my heart bleeds with many emotions, I write my worries away, taking a strong dose of gratitude.

# Day Nineteen

Have we been waiting?

Since schools have been out? Since we were told to stay home?
Since we last shopped at our favorite store?
Have we been waiting for all of this to be over? To eat out at
restaurants again? To visit the library? To meet our friends and
family?
I tend to get stuck in the mindset of waiting.
But then I remind myself, in waiting for the storms to pass, life
continues.
Even while we wait for the quarantine to be over, life is not
stopping.
The days of this year will forever be marked by days in quarantine,
but also as weeks of our lives that will never return.
It's not like months from today we can rewind the tape and start
back from March 12, 2020, the day our state reported its first case of
COVID19.
All this time in the meanwhile, in quarantine, still counts as life.

It's as much a part of our existence as the days we spent getting kids
ready and dropping them at school.
As real as those family get-togethers or dinners out with friends.
As much a part of our living as gleefully walking into Target and
seeing the new knick-knacks at Bullseye's Playground. I miss that
too.

But here's the thing: life is still unraveling every second of every day.
Either it could be spent waiting for all the dynamics to line up as
they used to, or it could be spent living in the now.
The now that requires a new approach in a new world. New
moments of glee must be found. Meaning needs to be redefined.
Because waiting lets moments pass as though there is no worth in
them.
There is no value in celebrating them.

Waiting makes us hunger for a future that only exists in our minds.

I am reminding myself regularly to not be stuck in the waiting game.
That these days, this age, this phase in my children's lives will never
come back.
That even in quarantine, while staying in place, the beauty of life
and existence remains.
I cannot be waiting for life to start back up again—it never really
stopped.

# Eyes Up

keep eyes up
searching
as steps transcend from
the daze of fluorescent skies
to thick draped ones

cloaks that guard
luminous light
full of wonder, hope
the ever-existent moon
clouded in heavy black

keep looking
without defeat
it remains
promising better tomorrows
than today

# Day Twenty

We are all survivors... survivors of our own individual circumstances.
Right now, we are all surviving this global pandemic in our own way.
Some of us are surviving the sickness itself.
Some are surviving after losing a loved one.
This is their journey, their survival.
We are ever grateful we are not sick or afflicted by the sickness, but
we are surviving our own circumstances.

Some of us are surviving being parents to little ones without any
help or relief.
Some of us are surviving being away from family members we
cannot see or meet.
Some are surviving jobs that force us into public spaces amid the
fear of getting sick.

All in survival mode. All different circumstances. All valid.

These are uncharted waters that none of us have been trained to
ride.
We are all in ships of our own, learning to steer and operate in the
best way that we can.
Different boats, different currents, the same water.
We are all trying to keep the shore in focus so we may dock our
ships successfully.

Unfortunately, some ships will never reach the shore... their ship is caught in choppy waters that are difficult and unpredictable.
We ache for them, we pray for them.
But the rest of us are trying to ride through our own circumstances.
We are all trying to make it through. We are all holding on.

We are all survivors.

# Day Twenty-One

There is beauty in the darkness of the night.
It doesn't make the bright skies of the morning any less or more beautiful.
Each one has a beauty unique to itself.

Incomparable.

I am more drawn to the beauty of the darkness these days.
Something about finding myself in the darkest hour.
I sit alone in the hush and feel grounded in the moment.
I am not needed by anyone. I don't need to answer any tiny voices. I am only me.

Just me and the quiet still of the night.

A time I get to spend with the person who I haven't listened to all day long.
She brings her worries, I bring my fears. She brings her dreams, I bring my desires. She brings her thoughts, I bring my ideas. And together we make sense of it all.
We rest only after finding some peace together, knowing that we are okay.

And then I smile.

Because I know that these fragile moments of beautiful peace are under the guardianship of He who is closer to me than my own self. There is beauty in the darkness because these are my hours of solitude with myself under the refuge of His mercy.

# Gaze

I am gazing at the stars tonight
as they sparkle to us down below
I'm wondering what they see in us
if they know what we know

That today what glistens so brightly
tomorrow will dim away
that the light that dances tonight
will disappear by the start of the day

I am gazing at the stars tonight
in awe of where they reside
dark curtains without wrinkles
content that they always hide

stars only glow bright and full
when darkness becomes their frame
they both depend on each other
but only one gets all the fame

I am gazing at the stars tonight
I wonder if they wonder the same

# Week Four

# Dusk

let dusk enter the windows
    and sit in the horizon awhile
birthed from the glory of a new day
    buried under the majesty of the night
let dusk emerge from between the two
    illuminate in its theatrical debut
as rays perform in bright hues
    spectacular as it fades too soon
memorialized in the twilight hour
    forgotten under the brilliance of the moon

# Day Twenty-Two

The days are passing, aren't they?

The impossible days you thought were too difficult to live through,
but you are, aren't you?
Living through them?
Going through that time period in your life you will one day reflect
on, thinking "How did I do it?"
"How did I live through the global pandemic of 2020?"
"Not leave my house for days on end?"
"Yet get up every morning and get the job done?"
"Plan and prepare in an age of fear?"
"How did I survive those uncertain times?"

"How did I do it all?"

The days are here and you are living through that historic moment
in your lifetime. The one you will always look back on.
"What did I learn from it?"
"What did I miss the most?"
"What did my quarantine time allow me to do that I couldn't have
done otherwise?"

The moments that redefine us are the chapters we choose as stakes
to mark the cornerstones in our lives. They are ones we will always
remember.

As reminders, to navigate ourselves through the hurdles of the future.

As guideposts, to impasse wisdom on ourselves in dark and difficult times.

Days will pass as they were designed to... sunsets that lead to sunrises that lead to sunsets again.

But these passing days in quarantine could be a chapter of reformation if we choose them to be.

If we have been seeking it.

The chapter that changed us for the better.

Years from now when you think back and reflect on these days, will you remember the chapter that defined a story, or stray pages that could've been?

# My Lord

Indeed, my Lord has spoken,
He needn't rely on speech,
With one single command,
The world fell to its knees.

Humbled by its fragility,
It has seen the might of He,
To whom belongs His creation,
Everything in its entirety.

He sends down upon us,
That which the eyes can't see,
It steals each breath silently,
No other remains but He.

I have seen my Lord's whispers,
On the earth I travel and roam,
But never before this clearly,
As inside the confines of home.

There is no mistaking His message,
He has made it abundantly clear,
When He speaks, the eyes listen,
He does not rely on ears.

Indeed, My Lord has spoken,
Speech that unfolds His decree,

That mankind should be caged in walls,
And the birds may be let out free.

Indeed My Lord, I hear You,
In the seen and in the unseen,
May my heart always listen,
live and die upon your *deen*.

# Day Twenty-Three

*Allah* told us our days would be numbered.

There have never been any surprises in His plan.

He never decreed that those who lived well or lived largely would be transformed into immortal beings.

His plan has always been the same. For everyone.

No king was able to buy more time. No peasant pleaded his way into forever.

He has fulfilled His promise every single time. Billions and billions of times.

That with every birth will come death. With every inhale, there will be an exhale. Every dawn will see dusk.

We accept the expiry of everything. Time. Food. Seasons. Animals. Years. Everything.

Everything but ourselves.

Somehow when it comes to ourselves, we are caught surprised.

Shocked by the suddenness. Knowing our finality but refusing to accept it.

The only elements we do not know about death is when it will arrive and in which packaging.

There is a mindset that only the elderly should be prepared for death.

However, is that because we expect those who have lived for a while to be ready to pack their bags, or because we keep wanting to push death further back from our own lives?

Why were we more at ease when we heard that this virus would be dangerous for only the older population?

And so shocked when it has taken the younger and the healthy?

Wasn't death promised to everyone?

Truth is that just as soon as we are born we are inching towards death.

And between those moments is life.

It gives me greater resolve to live my days fully when I wholeheartedly accept that my days are finite.

This quarantine reminds me of stories told by terminal patients about how realizing their limited days revived their energy to live.

It puts into focus what is important. What is truly valuable. And what legacy I want to leave behind.

I am not sick nor terminal by a doctor's prognosis, but my time is limited as decided by my Creator.

This virus has come in the form of a notification to me—a reminder to live fully.

# Until

Until there is time,
There is time
Until there is life,
There is hope
Until there is darkness,
There is light
Until there is pain,
There is healing
Until there is sadness,
There is joy
Until there is death,
There is life
Until there is time,
There is time

# Day Twenty—Four

Ever woke up to a morning after a night of rainfall?
I just did.
I didn't see it with my own eyes but there are reminders of it
everywhere.
The glistening road still soaked by the rain that fell upon it
relentlessly.
The trees that drip with beads of water. I imagine how they held
their ground under waves of rain, swaying with the wind but never
breaking.
The earth is rich with as much moisture as it can bear. It's arms
overflow with the weight of the downpour.
I can hear faint drops pittering into leftover pools of water that the
heat is still toiling to evaporate.
They still hold the rain in their hands... the drops keep adding to
their load.

I woke up from my slumber unaware that the night past had
weathered rains and winds.
Scattered reminders outside my window are storytellers revealing
the unfolding of the night.
As I peer at the sky, I see thick clouds retreating back into the crack
of the horizon.
Giving way to the sun.

And I am taken aback.

Taken aback by how the world is an art in motion.

The parallels between its unspoken poetry and the theatrical performance of life are undeniable.

I take in the dark night of rain, and the glorious morning after, and reflect.

How the current storms passing overhead will surely leave behind marks of when they once existed.

There will be grief and pain. Loss and fear. Worry and tears. The reminders will remain.

But there will come a sunrise. From the other side of the night, there will come a morning.

There will be a day after.

And maybe the heat of the day will eventually evaporate the remnants left behind, but the trees will tell you...

The soaked grass will remind you...

The dripping beads of water will whisper to you...

that the very rain that leaves behind scars from its wrath is the same one that feeds the earth so that it may blossom.

# A Letter to My Children

If I shall not wake, my dear,
Pray for me but do not fear
I only returned to where I belong,
We knew this hour would come along

I went to the loving embrace of He,
He called me home so I can be
Away from the trials that caused me pain,
But I see now that it was not in vain

I'll be sleeping now a slumber deep,
In the blanket of a fragrance sweet
The bed may be made of rocks and dirt,
But here there's no such thing as hurt

Wide and soft like a floating cloud,
No disturbing sounds, nothing loud
Just the hymns of those who sing His praise,
The heart of my soul does the same

I am at peace, where I'm meant to be,
Bound no more, forever free
I wish I'd kissed you one last time,
Your warm face resting next to mine

I may not tuck you in at night,
But let faith in Him hold you tight

In His name will be the place of peace,
Your sadness will go, your fears will cease

Carry on as life moves ahead,
Let thoughts of me not fill your head
My love will always be so near,
If I shall not wake, my dear

# Day Twenty-Five

I spend many nights thinking that I will succumb to my anxiety-ridden death as I fall asleep.
Which of course only increases my insomnia.
There I am alone in the dark, listening to the rhythmic ticking of my wall clock, a sound I rarely notice during the day.
Laying on my side, nestled under the covers, my mind wanders.
Are the doors locked? Was that the baby? What should I make for breakfast? Darn, I forgot to defrost the chicken so I could marinate it for dinner tomorrow!

And then the other thoughts infiltrate...

If something happens to me, who would take care of the kids? What if something happens to my husband? Is this tightness in my chest a heart attack? What if...? How would...?
Simple scenarios play out into tragic circumstances.
Imaginations turn into nightmares.
Heart thumping fast. Hands jittery. Body tense. Eyes open.
My bed is no longer a nest of comfort.

There I am, alone in my wakefulness with a house full of people, as my heart and mind mutually decide that they will succumb to panic.

I lay on my pillow and surrender.
I speak to God in that moment and ask Him to forgive me.
I ask him to give me ease. To protect my family. I ask Him for mercy.

I make peace with myself. I make peace with Him.

And right there, the panting, the thousand worries, the endless possibilities of things going wrong come to an abrupt stop.

I read my prayers. I imagine His magnificent presence.

I feel seen. I feel loved.

I am comforted in my peaceful surrender.

Before I know it, my eyes awake and it's 6 a.m.

I feel a rush of love and gratitude. I thank God for waking me from my slumber as I get out of bed.

Day after day, I feel like a dying person getting another chance.

It's not anxiety that I succumb to, but faith that I surrender to when I go to sleep.

## Succumb to Thee

if I succumb to thee
do not take me for weak,
I submit to His decree
the One I serve and seek

your power is only as great
as He wills it to be,
if that power plucks out my soul
I will surrender willingly

I am at my Master's call
whatever He decides it to be,
and if His loving words call for me
I shall succumb with joy to thee

# Day Twenty-Six

Shut the windows.

Lock the doors.

Draw the curtains.

Close the blinds.

Store your provisions.

Sit still.

It lingers outside like an invisible wind.
They used to say it can only affect you if you touch it but now they say it lurks in the unseen.

And when it gets you in its grips, it takes your breath away.

It sits heavy and sits deep.
It has left bustling streets barren. Congested cities abandoned. It has barred the entire world from roaming freely.

Fear.

The bold colors of fear have colored the virus a striking hue.
Yes, there is a virus that has been treacherous to whoever it meets.

But fear... fear has taken everyone as a prisoner.
Fear keeps you up at night. Fear heavies your heart. Fear makes you
buy more than you need. Fear makes you watch the news on repeat.
Fear of alerts. Fear of numbers. Fear of blaring ambulance sirens.
Fear of silence.
Out of all the elements that we cannot control, the one that we can,
has made us prisoners.

It is we who are making ourselves afraid.

We give fear the freedom to ravage our sanity by letting it take up
all the spaces of ourselves.
It snatches our sanity and peace of mind. And we allow it.
The virus may be incurable. But fear has an antidote. Fear has a cure.

It is hope.

As soon as we start exercising hope, it leaves fear winded... doesn't
it?!
The grip loosens. The heaviness lifts. The thickness becomes diluted.
Hope transforms soldiers into warriors. Transforms the dying, into
martyrs. Transforms the sick, into survivors.
Transforms ordinary stay-at-home mothers into enlightened poets.
Hope opens the windows and lets the sunshine filter in.
The virus has no cure, unfortunately. But fear does.
It is time to unearth hope from where we buried it deep in our
hearts like joy and optimism and peace and let it cast a spell over our
aching hearts.

It is time to shut fear out with hope.

# Prisoner

What if it seeps inside
Through the cracks of this fortress?

Where innocence still breathes
And joy echoes with delight?

It comes quickly I've heard
Like an air that forces change

And pulls at the threads of life
That cling to security

It lingers upon doorsteps
And creeps in uninvited

I am a prisoner, once free within walls
Now afraid to venture outwards

Into the jungles of demise
As it discovers what it seeks

Designed to overpower
All that it sees

While I am in here
A prisoner
To the unknown

# Day Twenty-Seven

A conversation:

The uncertainty is paralyzing.
"Tumkeen, you are not alone."

The virus keeps spreading every day.
"Tumkeen, you are not alone."

I haven't seen my parents, my brothers, and my sisters in months.
"Tumkeen, you are not alone."

I don't have any relatives near.
"Tumkeen, you are not alone."

My anxiety hits me in constant waves.
"Tumkeen, you are not alone."

I am grateful. I am fearful. I am hopeful. I am worried.
"Tumkeen, you are not alone."

The morning hustle doesn't rush me out the door anymore.
"Tumkeen, you are not alone."

At night, I lay awake unable to sleep.
"Tumkeen, you are not alone."

What if I get sick?
"Tumkeen, you are not alone."

What if someone in my family gets sick?
"Tumkeen, you are not alone."

What if I have to go to the hospital?
"Tumkeen, you are not alone."

What if it gets serious?
"Tumkeen, you are not alone."

And if I should die there?
"Tumkeen, you are not alone."

When they transport me to the graveyard?
"Tumkeen, you are not alone."

When I am buried by only strangers to fulfill my last rights?
"Tumkeen, you are not alone."

Alone in my graveyard with only me and my eerie silence...
"Tumkeen, you are not alone.... you never were."

# Soldiers

How do all the soldiers sleep?
with eyes heavy by what they've seen,
the images that stay and creep,
glances that close but never dream

How do all the soldiers sleep?
hour after hour on their feet,
their own fears they bury deep,
tireless pursuing victory

guarding the sick and the ones too weak,
holding their hands so they rest in peace,
eyes too sorrowed to even weep,
How do all the soldiers sleep?

# Day Twenty-Eight

*"...first time in American history all states are under an emergency declaration."*

This line from today's newspaper rings poignantly true.
It's the first time that what is happening to one is happening to the other.
It is the first time we are collectively battling a disaster.
We are united in our anguish and worry.

Together we are learning to understand what is and is not important.
The wealth that health truly is, and the privilege to have both.
A deep understanding of what it's like to be human.
That the human heart is not obliged to feel only one emotion at a time but can feel a spectrum of emotions simultaneously.
Every state is the same. Every American is the same.
We are not divided by our race here nor our status. Yes, some have felt the grip tighter than others but the choke is felt by all.
No citizen is immune. No immigrant is spared. No migrant can seek refuge from this virus.
There are no red states, blue states, or even green states here. Again, same.
At a time in history when we couldn't be more divided by our views, the virus has reminded us how same we actually are.
If we can grasp that concept right here, right now, regardless of the severity of this virus, we have won.
If we understand that the politicians and the policies that try to win by dividing us, only succeed if we choose to ignore that we are all more alike than we are different, then we are the victors. We have won as a people, as a nation, as humanity.

If a microscopic particle that is as invisible as air can remind us of our human condition, then why can't the eyes that can clearly see?

And like the poetic way God works, we are all uniformed to look just like one another now too.
For the first time in American history, we all look the same. The doctors and healthcare workers are in masks. The mailman and the grocery clerks are in masks. The lady at the bank is in a mask, and the woman walking her dog is in a mask.
Coast to coast, mountains to flat plains, cactus landscapes to pine tree fields, everyone and everywhere, all of us wear the same shields against the common enemy.
Our prayers are united, our struggles are parallel, and we all go to bed with that same fear etched on our foreheads.

At a time when sensitivity has been at its peak and the country has been so decisively divided, all states are waking up to this virus whispering what we long needed to hear:
that for the first time in American history, we are in this—all of us in all of this—together.

# Day Twenty-Nine

I stood in my shower this morning, in a rush to get my day started.
And then I stopped.
And stood still.

All of a sudden, I found myself taking a moment to take in the moment.

It was a childlike fascination, to be aware of the water I was standing under.
I allowed myself to feel the waterfall pour over my head and rush down my face.
I could feel it stream over my closed eyes, my nose, and down my chin, dripping to the floor.
I cupped the flowing water into my hands and splashed it over my face again, exhilarated by the rejuvenation I felt tingling from an awakened spirit.
I became present with the droplets fastened upon my rounded shoulders.
Energized by the water cascading down my back like the rush of a flowing river.
The rainfall from my shower hummed and the trickling from my body sounded like loose beads pattering against a tiled floor.
The faint aroma of cleanliness mixed with floral notes lingered throughout the air.

My heightened senses mapped the course of each droplet traveling down the landscape of my body, sparking wonder and exhilaration along the way.

At that moment, I drank in the moment.

It felt like the sea replenishing my parched soul.

Being present and aware felt a lot like gifts being unwrapped at the most unpredictable moments.

I find myself opening many such unexpected gifts these days.

It has awakened my soul to how truly breathtaking being alive is.

And how every moment is worth drinking in.

# End Note:

## A Reflection

# Always Remember

I will always remember,
that chilly day in March,
3:45pm,
when they came home with bags packed full,
and a weary look,
of those who await in trenches,
for the storm that sits on the horizon.

when uncertainty rang bells of worry,
and in droves some hoarded mundane items.
when we made lists for provisions,
and medications,
and pointed out the files of documentation,
to a child who understood implications,
of "just in case...".

when we went to sleep forgiving one another,
and told each other our last wishes.
when we witnessed people drop like flies,
news spitting out numbers, like they had no names.
when freezer trucks lined parking lots,
and tents were propped up,
and venues meant for celebrating,
shifted into gatherings of a somber kind.

when everyone stepped out in coverings,
and it became the norm,

and the respectful, honorable thing to wear.
like those who had done so previously,
but were met with hesitation,
fear of that which couldn't be understood.
now they understand preservation,
protection and commitment,
but they'll never admit it,
because we are cut from a cloth of a different kind.

when city streets became barren battlefields,
homes became fortresses,
and cars sat empty with nowhere to go.
when schools sat eerily empty,
yet the sounds of laughter and bells,
rang inaudible in the wind that blew past them.
when parks become play less,
shops sat moneyless,
and the hustle of the everyday,
stopped at the signal that had no one to direct,
and nowhere to go.

when the first signs of spring,
had birds chirping in the far distance,
as ambulances blared in the early morning,
starkly reminding others,
of the perils hidden behind large glass doors.
as we all impatiently stayed home,
there were brave soldiers lined up,
row upon row upon row,
barely shielded gallants,

who braced the harsh heat,
and stood for hours on their feet,
armed with thermometers, ventilators, and tubes for air.
where we left our sick to be mended,
and the dying at the mercy of those who held them,
away from loved ones at home.


when houses of God locked their doors,
and the call to prayer was altered,
and congregations were told to worship at home.
when the Mecca of worship,
no longer gathered congregants,
gates became shuttered,
and tiled floors were seen for the first time.
when brotherhood and community were nowhere to be found,
lots sat empty on days of rejoice,
and lectures from the couch just weren't the same.
when the congregation of a family unit united,
as we prayed together, longer,
and learned to collectively understand,
how mighty the word of God is,
and how He was the only One in control.
how buildings did not hold faith, people did.
how holy days were righteous by those who preserved them.
when we realized faith didn't rest on pillars,
but was upheld by those who held it sacred.
like a roof that shelters,
but does not stop,
the coming of a devastating disaster.

when we stayed home,
together, families ate meals.
they read books,
they walked and played,
made and stayed,
worked and learned,
together.
laughter lingered longer,
love seeped deeper,
eyes were engaged,
hands were held,
and hugs sat long enough to become warm.
when joy was discovered within hearts,
and in small moments of being gathered under one roof,
nothing was loaned,
nothing was lent,
and all happiness came from within.
when we were awakened to what was missing,
and we discovered that the most precious gifts,
are the free ones.
like time,
health,
love,
family,
faith,
and joy,
but they desired and required to be acknowledged.

when the entire world and all the billions that reside here,
became one concerned family.

there was nowhere that was safe,

nowhere to run to,

no refuge nor safe space,

and the common enemy that war was being waged against,

was an invisible agent, unseen to the naked eye.

how we weren't really at war...

if we were, both sides would have a chance for victory.

no, it was the one ravaging us,

With endless relentless force.

we were powerless,

with all our weapons,

and ammunition,

and money,

and technology,

and prestige,

we were powerless.

No, it was a one-sided attack,

all we could do was hide and wait,

and pretend like we had any capability at all.


I will remember the lists of numbers.

how many people,

how many sick,

how many died,

how many hours,

how many weeks,

how many beds,

how high the temperature,

how many machines,

which countries,

which cities,
the percentages,
the rates,
the stocks and the oil,
the unemployment and the assistance.
prices. checks.
I will remember the numbers and the data.
and how presumptions and models,
became the all-knowing, all-aware,
and all people believed in were numbers,
or rage against them.
numbers became trusted entities,
and a hated enemy,
but all agreed,
that numbers never lie.

I will remember the baking.
the endless cooking,
the teaching that tried the patience of my being.
in the mission to fill up days,
books were picked up,
board games were dusted,
meetings were zoomed,
connections became virtual,
and sightseeing happened from the screen of a phone.
matches were postponed; appointments were canceled;
commitments just went away.
calendars became clean slates,
urgency vanished,
and life became an empty canvas of stay.

I will remember how the world changed,
and our lives changed,
though we were still all the same.

how our minds changed,
and our schedules changed,
but what was important still remained.

I will remember witnessing time stand still,
and the desperation of the incurable ill,
but the human condition stayed the same.

I will remember breathing a little deeper,
sleeping a little longer,
but the days and hours were still the same.

butterflies awoke, grass rebirthed,
plants grew buds then transformed to leaves,
and how the seasons went and came.

I'll remember watching life from inside windows,
and marveling over sunrises and starry nights,
falling in love with the simple, like a child again.

I will remember how the fragility of life,
the healing power of faith,
and death waiting outside my door,
taught me empathy for all,
beauty in the everyday.

to be alive and to live are not the same.

reminders flicker for only a while,
so I'll be grateful for the now,
and relish the light as long as I can,
before the extinguishment of this unforgettable flame.

# Glossary

**Allah** - God

**Deen** - A Muslim way of life that adheres to Islamic laws, beliefs, customs, and deeds

**Eid** - a holiday celebrated by Muslims twice a year. *Eid ul Fitr* is celebrated at the end of Ramadan (month of fasting) and *Eid ul Adha* celebrated in the month of Dhul Hijjah (month of pilgrimage)

**Jummah** - Arabic word for Friday (a day when Muslims pray together in congregation)

**Quran** - the Holy book revealed to Prophet Mohammed (PBUH)* by Allah through the Angel Jibraeel that Muslims follow and believe in

**Masjid** - a place of worship for Muslims; also referred to as Mosque

**Sunnah** - following the example and practices of the Prophet Mohammed (PBUH)*

*PBUH  - peace and blessings be upon him

# Acknowledgements

I would like to first and foremost thank Allah for guiding my heart and pen in the way that brings joy and solace no matter where I am or how. I would also like to thank my coach and friend Na'ima B Robert who dared me to dream and trained me to make it come true. To my editor, Hend Hegazi, for the support, and encouragement with a firm "Bismillah" whenever I needed it. Thank you to Susie Poole for making my vision for this book come to life. To all the incredible women I have met throughout this past year, your words and support spoke to my heart and gave this book the courage to leap. To my loves, thank you for believing for me when I couldn't myself; there's no one else I would be in a pandemic lockdown with than with you.

# About the Author

Tumkeen is an author, contributing writer, and poet. She resides in the northern suburbs of Detroit, Michigan with her husband and children. Her work has been published in numerous publications, blogs, and websites. She draws inspiration from her faith, family, and the natural elements around her. Tumkeen candidly describes her writing journey as "I am writing to heal, and healing to write". She enjoys watching the sun rise every morning, creating memories with her children, and spending time with loved ones.

Tumkeen
Writer + Poet

Made in the USA
Columbia, SC
31 January 2021